AN IOTA
OF POMES

AN IOTA
OF POMES

– ON EARTH PLANE COMPLEX –

CHARLES D HELT

a search for reason & meaning
&
this is what happened

Pomes = just plain ole flat poems
47 = all racecars

poetry is
an abstraction
of the star's
light
bent to where
you see
an iota...

& a
little more...

MOBIUS POEMS

a man
in his earthly trek
confronted his mobius form
extending in all directions
from his hand

he rubbed his finger
along the curved edge
& suddenly became conscience
of karma & god is not dead

a man
in his earthly trek
saw once a mobius strip
as the path he was upon

pausing,

he saw the strip expand
beyond the factories & beyond the sun
expanding all the way into
the narrow path
this universe is upon

POND

a pond
is a system of molecules
each entwined
being little bit
weird
yet uniquely
forming
each little bit
of universe
on its
own

a pond
is alone
as an individual
cavity
within the dirt
of earth
& yet life
teams
from its insides
& speaks of
hope
from its
molecules

POETS JUMP

poets jump
'round the mountains
scientist discuss
that very mountain
religion speaks
'bout knowing mountains
who has seen
that ole mountain

three years into the future
people remember now

trees & flesh survive somehow

ever seen universe
described in a moment

ever notice continuity
extends into vastness

ever notice the strings
attached to your atoms

ever understood
you know not even an iota

whoever climbed
a mountain
he didn't respect
afterwards

Plot Thickens

& so
the plot thickens
& thusly
begins the task
so long awaited

interior depths
quantities known
now inherent
let it flow

in harmony
two plus two
is greater than four
synergism is a force

& on earth
a spot in universe
there is treachery
there is deception
all entwined
with a little harmony

i want
a flicker of hope
a dot of truth
solitude
something good
& you

DIMENSIONALLY SPEAKING

once upon earth was found
this odd molecular bond
of quarks & atoms moving
in a cohesive consistent conscious creature

which somehow i intelligently
nominated as me, myself, & i.

one of us in here was wondering aloud
just what is this stuff in which we are found
comprehending aspects as right from wrong
subjective vs objective
existence & infinity

just who do you think you are
oh little one on earth growing
to be in the image
of understanding we are not
what we think we see

rather we come & go in reality
like quantum entanglement w/ duality
sometimes here, sometimes there,
sometimes everywhere or nowhere
as particles or waves

spinning in thickened waters
of the tiniest so small
in this vastness of it all

sensation of consciousness
stranger than the reality
we think we see

IF YOU DON'T ENTER THE RACE

there's another way to hell
& on the other side
you're alone in your boat
paying for the ride

reduce the problem bring it inside
deduct the quotient what's alongside
the remainder is your reminder
you're such a rookie driver
not even a chance to ever understand

if ya don't ever question or wanna know why
if ya don't enter the race
why do you survive

BLACK HOLE

like
talking to a black hole
the words circle the surface
with only tidbits of response
tantalizing communication
in less than a flash of a moment
like
talking to a black hole
thinking it is the center of the galaxy
when in reality
it's
not even there

BALLYHOO

"rock 'n rollin' now boys"
his neatly cut freshly pressed suit
his perfect cherry wood desk
sharpened with corporate credentials
"rock 'n rollin' now boys"
like the illogical vote
to cut the poor man's chances
so the broke & poor can sing more blues
while the cherry desk feels his money
grown on the dead coral in the once thriving sea he's killing

ONE DOLLAR

a dollar bill
lying crumpled
next to another
dollar bill
lying all crumpled
reminds quite well
of current concept
of american dream

EXPONENTIAL

as the numbers get higher
unit by unit increasing one per time
the significance of change decreases
from the massive height
of one hundred percent at two
thru the half quantity change at three
to the infinitesimal small change
of one at a trillion
does anyone feel the same

THE HAPPENING

a tree swing
on its arc's apex
broke
& left
a thousand people
rebuilding

THIRTY-FIVE CENTS PLEASE

little lady strolled the bakery
of subtleness & thought
& bought
incorrect concepts
as freshly made pastry

INDECISION

indecision
is the wrong
decision

yet with precision
wrong decisions
can be
right decisions

WEIRDED M'SELF

weirded out m'self
today at the track
saw the phase of reality
fade in & come back
could almost see around the corner that wasn't
there

watched the oddness of transparency
wobble in structural matter
as i walked thru the gate
the realness of grand luminous reason
spoke & poked & pointed to wisdom
not always in a normal place
unless you look

REALITY SCREEN

fragile
so very short

time so vast
space expanding

momentarily an iota
so very fragile

earth plane complex
this existence

reason & meaning
vastly unseen

finitely flashed
on reality screen

so very short
feel the consciousness

truth exponentially
oddly revealing

so very fragile
earthly existence

earth time
be here now

OLD HOUSE BY THE SIDE OF THE ROAD

instantly
thoughts congregated
on the memories of festivals long gone
of christmas & thanksgiving
of easter & birthdays
of barefoot cousins running
catching fireflies in bottles
& parents bragging
on how much the kids had grown

little remains of that old house
the one over there
broken roof
unpainted
dilapidated
falling down completely
returning back to earthly soil

so many life filled stories
worthy of books of life well written

EACH DAY

this could be the last time
the final time
the end of times
of your times
this could be the last time

drove a nail today
walked a block or two
said i love you to you
filled the gas tank too
this could be the last time

the crawling credentials
of existence
eventually collides
in reality particle accelerators
revealing all kinds of you

this won't be the last
of you

THEY'VE GOTTA LEARN

some folk seem to think
they are more correct
than anyone else...

when in reality
it is myself
who is the most correct
of everyone else...

EPITAPH

attention span
diversions
can take a brief
dot in time
& turn it into
a lifetime
in no time at all

WE BELOW

the ice flows
as the sun glows
& we below
want to know
why

BE NOT TARDY

spin on earth
ride it to heaven

say howdy
for me
& likely

in reality

being on time
is tardy

OCCASIONALLY

I've had more fun
in a dentist chair
than the sunrise to sunset
events of
this beautiful sky blue
spring day
today

ANTIQUITY

watched this stuff
from the days of youth
become an antique show
worth less than before
to anyone else
but me

MENTALITY

evolution
has not occurred
in the dinosaur mentality
being presented
as everyday
knowledge
today

THIS MOMENT

momentarily
we are
who we are

then we will
be ourselves
differently

momentarily
tomorrow
occurs

it takes a lifetime
to know
this moment in time

IF The door opened left
The Word on The STREET
Would be
it was BACKWARDS

The blue sky he said
oh Don't be silly
'tis grey & cloudy

Each Atomic destiny
free willfully thrives
'ceptin' yours
Through Anothers eyes

19

STILL INTERESTING

how events bite back many years later
a thought from the olden thinking something was
absurd
is so logical
when the vice squeezes new directions

SMILINGLY

smilingly she
spit disrespect
as she shook my hand
& said
I am here
for the good
of the clan

RATTLESNAKE RECIPE

catch snake by the tail…
swing it around & around…
then with a quick whip-snap…
remove the head…

simmer bones
in white mirepoix
for stock…
add roux for a veloute based sauce…
season with tobasco & cayenne…

sauté meat…
delicately…
in cilantro flavored olive oil…

serve over breadcrumbs
sautéed to the appearance
of sand…
garnish with pickled cactus…

make belts from skin & rattles…
total utilization….

sell belts in craft shows
on weekends…

reserve venom for medical use…

catch another…
do it again….

INITIAL AWARENESS OF VASTNESS

geometric? no, translate: personified;
visual? yes, classify: colored thought;
synthesize
the
way
all things change
a magical ocean in worldly motion
a tropical river in lovely realms
& crack
a quiet sound is heard amongst the trees
a universal order is dwelled in your realm
a thicket of peace encompassing all can be seen
&
color
sparkling unseen & meaning the dream
is reached by the color of thought
so infinitely vast
mentioned you
quite a view

QUEST UPGRADE

really want to know
how the soul
strolls
with the strings
of quantum & gravity

SOLITUDE

occasionally recuse
yourself
from being a recluse

isolation
is of use

but there is a time
to be of use
elsewhere

A CONSCIOUS DECISION

a brain cell
receives
instructions to vibrate electrons
bringing structured
procedures
to the other electrons
in your body
to begin
altering
your present
concept of reality
by use
of your physical extremities

so what
essence of you
started the electrons
moving
in the first place

ONE OH FOUR ON ELEVEN TWENTY-TWO IN SIXTY-THREE

who would shoot
the janitor i thought
he's a nice man
i'm in jr high but still
he's a nice man
who would shoot
the janitor i thought

one oh four after lunch
industrial arts classroom
intercom speaker blared
facing south in the building
age of reason ascending
who would shoot
the janitor i thought

just saw him yesterday
in that small closet
khaki pants mop in hand
taking care of our school
mr kennedy was nice
who would shoot him i thought

just didn't seem right
until i found out
it was not the janitor
but another mr kennedy
just didn't seem right
just didn't seem right
just didn't seem right

TIM & I

the back door opens
we looked thru
centuries
since we last played

ten foot kites
mouse over the house
mice launched so high
some of them survived
estes model rockets

slot cars home-made all
rebuilt
piece by melted broken
piece
rocket cars on strings
his attic above the garage
cigarettes lit by sneaking
in jr high teachers un-
locked cars

just kids in the sixties
pushing technology
& other things
never afraid

homemade weak gun
powder
failed luckily
in orange juice tin cans
with holes in the bottom
topped with soldered
pointed-nose cones

stayed friends all those
years
his used cars, my tax
returns
we both knew
we knew what went on

we talked one last time
fifty plus years later
both knowing
what was probably coming

the mouse rocket had to
land sometime
we had taken the space
race most seriously
as pre-teen boys in the
early sixties

AREN'T YOU?

when walking with you
at the grocery store or the racetrack
quantum & time may actually have
the two or parts of us
in other places this very moment
in time

maybe more

& though I'm with you
doing things with you
walking the sidewalk with you
I am trying to see through
the oh so famous wording
of fabric of space & time

aren't you?

WORK DAY READY

new office chair in site
work day ready
morning coffee brewed
problems to solve
laid out like jigsaw puzzles
sorted & ready
to go together
but i
want my electric blanket
crawl back under
watch tv
can't breathe
no energy
durn cold

TRUE STORY 'TIS THIS

to my right wing brethren
i said last night
let's stop the venom
& hatred
& be american
with differences no doubt

he said he'd have to get back to me
on that one

ANOMALY?

todays thought process
begins
do not do the normal

TO VICKY

right exactly when
i put the last piece
in this second
thousand piece
jig saw puzzle stack
the electricity blinked
then went off
then came on
& the light bulb in the lamp
on the table next to my chair
popped -
then popped again
& Bronco barked
& Jeremiah jumped
right up into
the middle
of the puzzle
which caused the table
to meet the floor.

luckily,
after mixing up both puzzles
they went together
rather quickly

upside down
& backwards

TODDLER'S LEARN (OUR TURN)

a toddler learns to walk
by falling down
& gets mad &
throws a tantrum fit

yet learns to walk
amongst others
without knocking them over
most of the time

should not earth
have learned
war
the same way?

BULLS PLAY HOCKEY

wires & paper
engulf the day
tangled & woven
massive display

paper free society
wireless society
set us free
bull hockey

40,000

Forty thousand people
without electricity
but all i want to see
is the power back on
for my one t.v.

THE PLANE RIDE

she spoke of as sacred
let her landing gears touch down
on something far away from actuality

& NO

& no
no organized organization
holds this fascination
very long

& no
no science nor religion
speaks all truth
nor fiction

& no
no I just won't go
over there
again

ASK HER

the only reason
i evolved arms
is to
pet my cat
in the mornings

ask her...

BEING

when ten years
is less than a snap
of the fingers

when re-memory
blushes yesterday
as a decade

we easily see
the vastness
of continuity

we see how
centuries are
daily flashes

eons
mere dots &
hyphenated dashes

the Ultimate
much more
than irrelevant

LIFE

life
life style
life moving
life changing
life long friends
life partner forever
life everlasting loves
life time my lifetime is
life before me after me
life family inspiration
life living sensation
life grandness is
life texture for
life lesson
life goal
life is
love

CRUSHED STEEL

foreboding
lies heavy heartfelt today
as crushed steel & dreams
compacted for throw away

know not why
fully at least
but doing less than the best
i could've
not being able to help
where i could've if i would've

probably have lain open my dreams
to be like crushed steel
piercing heavy in
the heart today...

SWIM FASTER

the last particle in the universe
waited
to finish the idea
just a little further from the shore
than it began

TALL OAK

tall oak well formed
imperfectly sprouted
near four other tall oaks
scattered across pristine winter grass
expressing the randomness
of beauty & pretty reality
chaos in formation
perfectly
revealing
their cells & quarks
behaving in natural law & patterns
of mathematically ordered chaos
exponentially large
infinitely small
& much
weirder
than you ever
imagined

OIL

takes a long time
to form
"but we don't know
how long Adam lived anyway"
he said
defending his long term investments

another chip of intolerance
displaying
its granite of impenetrable
close mindedness

creationists
give us all
blackened eyes

STEEP STAIRS

going down those long steep stairs was easy
looking up from the bottom is perplexing
how this happened
does not matter
because it did happen

the inner quark knew
long before
the outer quark admitted

HENRY DAVID DOTH PROTEST

privacy
as Thoreau hidden
is forbidden
with
cell phones around

ELIXIR

the first little lie
revealed how easy it was
& gullible they are

the second lie
covered the first
under so much misdirection
questioning on the first lie ended
because it was too far in the past…

the third lie was really two more
misdirection's on opposite sides
until the truth originally hidden
was now totally re-written…

by the time of the forty seventh lie
there were so many turns & mazes
ropes & dangling phrases
no one even remembered
all this started
with one little lie

MICROWAVE TIME

door shut, buttons punched
beep beep beep hummmmmm
forty-seven seconds
hot dog nice & warm
microwave warm

but

where did you spend
your precious seconds
in mind & thought

where was your consciousness

was it forty-seven seconds lost
spent in a mush

or did you contemplate the
vastness of space & the tiny
atomic particles moving & heating
that little ole hot dog you're about
to wrap in cheese, add mustard, & eat

GETS IT I NEEDS IT

more...
always want more...
more of this
more of that
excess
abusive excess
two for the price of one
larger size please make it bigger
always want more...
why reach for a single universe
when more are available
get more
want more
gets it
i needs it...

A PAIR OF KITTENS

Sufi & Spooky
Spunky & Slinky
Respectively,
Slipped & Slid Screamingly
Sideways & Seemingly Slowly
Simply into Slumber

CORPORATE JOB

i'm a cog
a machine type cog
see me turn
i'll turn as much as you want
see me move
oil me & i'll move some more
i'm a graphic digital copy
in a computerizing monopoly
see me turn
i'm a cog in a machine
watch me change
become a new model
see my paint
i change it every night
a plastic elevator manipulator
in a structural calculator eliminator
i'm a cog

WAVE MAKER

in thick liquid
pushing thru & walking
making waves & talking
moving in time fluidly
giving gravity
to mass

weight to existence

a spin pushing a
swimming pool wave

that's how it is
Higgs Boson
creating reality
in holographic ways

CLAY ASTEROIDS THAT MATTER

gonna be fun
in the Alternative Universe
wherein everything outside of here
contains No Matter

Chili Bowl Midget Nationals

a place where tires & rubber spin
in rotational severity
causing asteroids of clay
to fly from rear wheels
like the early earth in formation.

TAD GROUCHY

tad grouchy
tad touchy
tad roughly are ya
sure
'twas innocent
'twas self defense
'twas hardening inability of control
'twas reaction to inept decisiveness
tad grouchy
tad touchy
'tis me

PROOF

The eyes of a cat
at play
is proof enough
eternal truth must be fun

Sun Glasses

like wearing glasses
darkened for the sun
hidden in a closet
with no light bulb on

yuppies & their children
forgot & did not teach
the utopian screams
of war baby boomer dreams

so after electing one
they elected another
& still fight
a war from long ago

like wearing glasses
darkened for the sun
in a torcher chamber
with no light bulb on

AROUND

instantly knew
the smiling smile
was really real
the very one
to take away
the days of fun

always knew
her soul was there
coming again
not wanting to end
like once before
good-bye old friend

'EH MR EISENHOWER

wooden stump
standing for a tree
long gone

reminds of
American peace
long gone

the culture
of war has been
fertilized

well seeded in our tree's fruit
& won't go away
anymore

military/industrial
complex
really happened

'eh mr eisenhower

OH WHENEVER

from the depths of wherever
to the realm of however
returned we for whatever
the weather may bring

deciding which is what
& for what reason
& why we are where
we are here where we are
is reason enough
to challenge
the day
fully

QUITE BLUNT

opined
did i
quite blunt
& got the brunt
of his
anxiety
run amuck

IT HAPPENS

we built on the glory
the monumental material glory
we trusted ignorance & fate
our misstance & non knowledge
we absorbed in the beauty
relished in the hope
& did not want what
we were after

we trust again in fate
non knowledge abounds
material monumental technicality
may lead beauty out
we again will build on glory
what is done shall return
non knowledge changes to hope
we were misled once
again though
we'll go after

BOX OF CHOCOLATES

wham bang rip the box is opened
displaying barely wrapped
morsels of chocolate
covering cherries melting
like perfect karma in aroma
allowing the hand
to quickly one by one
sometimes two by two
move the chocolate
the fourteen point seven inches
from table to mouth
usurping taste buds willfully
so fast the memory lasts
until the next morsel
& then it's over

CONGRESSIONAL TESTIMONY

got up, climbed the wall,
rode the reprehensible beast
climbed down, looked around
gathered wood for the feast

saw the witness lie today
lie like the truth was not ok
spun a yarn
worse than a dirty barn
claiming he stood for me
whether i knew it or not

BAYLEE

she was
stiff & upright
smiling, jovial, & bouncy,
standing on the street sign barricade
propped up by grandpa standing...
in strong anticipation
of event fascination...
then...
melting & limping all muscles
relaxed...
as Santa Claus walked by...

CHAIN REACTING

tumbling 'round the tube of known life
the ball is oiled for smooth rolls
over the jumps the bumps the ball is oiled
here it goes...

in the morning
awakening to the alarm by music
the soft gentle rolls of rock rhythm
  the lamp cord is pulled by a foot
    in its wild attempt to find the floor
      the noise awakens the dogs
      who bark & chase off
      the beauty birds who sing
      on peaceful mornings,
        the birds fly to the roof
        landing on the loose hail damaged ventilation vent
      which falls
        politely & quietly
        on the well abused ford mustang
        which pops the gear shift out of park
      & rolls smoothly into the garage door
which being well oiled
    uncoils its spring in a mighty twang
    flies through the project room door
      & into the kitchen
    smashing the stove which has breakfast cooking
    which causes the hot spilled cooking oil
    to run smoothly slowly steadily
      through the dining room down the hall
    through the bedroom door & onto the very spot
    where the other wildly placed foot
    is just coming down.

LONELY ROAD

on a lonely road through the
abyss of a time warp, i saw
a glaring white glow beckoning
my body onward. this ole
road was paved in mud &
blood, no gold around, so
the body knew the road was
earths mode towards the
end of time, & many of
the previous travelers had
long died & turned to
mud. still, unafraid,
'cept of my own ineptitude, i
kept my eye on the glaring
white glow, trudged on,
& became dirty & dirtier
& dirtier, finally concluding
earth was meant to make
one dirty & the glow
to beckon
you on

STARKNESS

the starkness of the flower
against the white wall background
pink & purple & green colors forthright
we all have a right
to life & death on this earth plane complex

a most important day of life since birth
her atoms seek the earth
her molecules have the oxygen of freedom breathed
& now like all she must leave
& seek the universe beyond

a life is the time preceding death
a life is the short time we have
confused, disillusioned, & complex,
hopeful, loving, & a learning experience,
Please say hello for us when you get there.

CLICHÉ SO QUIT DIGGING

a man
on the run
for fun
met himself
in a ditch
filled with water
& understood
he dug the hole
& supplied the water
& conceives a wooden raft
to float upon
if he'll build it

SNOW

snow falling
reminds of
orderly chaos
in continuity
from vast system
to beyond & within
quantumly
mathematically
letting
randomness
occur
orderly
naturally

UNDEFINED FLOWER OF FIG

unrefined, undefined,
in the raw state of being,
we see, we think, we somehow
believe in the garden of our birth
that we each alone is the best,
the most refined, defined,
citizen on god's green & blue earth.

we cannot be hurt
for he himself was given for us

he must have noticed
for the earthquake was over there;
the tornado was in another city;
the tsunami missed us completely.

"Yes sir, those folks over there they knew better
Must've been their sin
to put their life in such tatters!!!"

until within,
so deeply within
the garden of who you are,
grows a little flower
layered & blooming from inside out
like a fig in fresh tilled soil.

forgive, & admit;
accept, & repent;
you know not even an iota.

now you may grow.
...enjoy...

THEY TRIED

stab at my back
with a dagger of stature
rub on my neck
with the blood of slander
hunt in my yard
with the danger of canyons
walk in your yard
with the serpent animal

fill this ole earth
with ridicule & hatred
let everyone know
the dark sided behavior
have all the edges
razor sharp & lengthened
as for this ole earth
we knew you were coming

Electronic Device

need another device
electronic device
more wires please
charge my batteries
plug in my device
my electronic device
keep me going
up to date
version two point two
new charger please
upgrade my software
register my name
want another device
wireless electronic device
lots of wires please
plug in my device
extend my warranty
keep me up to date
need another device
one i can find
this time

PYRAMID

tall building touching sky
above the lights beautiful sight
bottom side peering sky height landing
pyramids Egyptian five thousand years
wonder if this one will be here then
williams center

NOPE

has an icicle ever felt
the summers breeze
& been at ease

UNEXPANDED

*unexpanded concepts of reality
really frustrate & limit
the unseen*

MoJo

with her life
privileged were
we entrusted

the purrs
  the cuddles
    the be real attitude
the softness
all entwined

there is nothing
quite like
knowing a kitten
through adult life

now she hurts
& we must do
an entrusted

thank you for
letting us be yours

stay gold
MoJo

THE PARADOX

we sat in the yard
discussing what we saw
with any who listened
we traveled the world
we explored in beyond
& came again to our source
loving the grass we sat upon

we mentioned the paradox
for in each paradox we walk
in each endeavor lies paradox
& the yard was pretty
as pretty as springtime green
but could not talk

we traveled thru time
twisted the mind to love
even when understood
we didn't understand & then
the sky got cloudy
& it rained, yet remained
a beautiful day

HELLUVATIME

you two get along now
'cause I won't be here
she said in her dying days
& it took a while
& a while longer
& maybe not exactly
but we did
as she said
& had a
helluvatime
helluvatime
having a helluvaGoodTime
he said last summer
at the racetrack
with a sparkle in his blue eyes

SADNESS

more than deeply
compressed in emotions
of earthly pangs
is depressed said i

get unfrozen
free will exists
choose to proceed
stop the frozen ice
clogging the veins
of wisdom & truth
please proceed

RESTRICTED WALKWAY

an eye for an eye
is so old testament

fundamentalism
restricts creation

science does not
dispel the you within

minds narrowed
subvert vastness

some rich folk
want poor folk

bronze age writings
misinterpretations

space flight waiting
those procrastinating

Infinite time
does not wait

infinity passes
this moment & again

A BOTTLE OF CATSUP PAGE 1

i opened the refrigerator door
a bottle of catsup
fell to the floor
my feet jumped up
but gravity pulled this body down
onto the broken glass
laying all around

screaming extremely loud
myself again jumped up
& did a flip
hitting the ceiling
with catsup drenched fist

now this squirrel in the attic
startled by these strange vibrations
escaped out through a vent
landing firmly on the roof
exactly where our outside cat
just happened to be napping

with wild eyes & fur flying
cat jumps from the roof
landing precisely
with claws outstretched
onto the enormous back
of our neighbors great dane dog

loud barks & screaming cat
dog chases cat
up this old dead tree
which then breaks a limb
which like a laser guided missile falls
onto the electrical line & pole

as the electrical line snaps
a back surge of power is sent into the city
causing just a momentary blink
all across town

& all those non power backed up
computer users
watch their lil ole computers
reboot & lose a little of their data
because of a bottle of catsup

save your work
bottles of catsup happen

BAD HABIT

boom
ka pow
aim straight down
bam
damn the foot
damn the toe
pistol shot
rifle shot
straight at the foot
ouch big toe
by thine own self
did the shot come
& keeps on
a-coming
shot m'self
in the foot
again

VASSAL

despair
terrible despair
she said telepathically
coming thru
quite clearly
to all
standing in the voting line
knowing their ballots
would be cast
for the very ones
who make them the least
among non-equals

Contemplative Communication

incredible incendiary emotion
invokes intensive excursions
into inner improvable explorations
extremely exclusive intrusions
entirely invisible
externally
'cept internally
instantaneously
enjoyable
& today

THIS

this technology
almost works
on both sides
of sanity

SO PROUD

peddle sewing machine
high tech of it's era
fed by the spinning wheel
finished by a wooden snap on button fastener

high tech of it's era
high tech of it's era
she was so proud
her family now clothed

the ice box arrived
wood stove to cook
garden out back
fresh milk delivered

high tech of it's era
high tech of it's era
she was so proud
her family now fed

LOW LEVEL

on a low level we
must remain
to gain for the peace
we proclaim
on a high level we
must situate
in ways of the love
we saturate

if a change we call for
must be made
& those in the world
seem afraid
on the highest level we
must remain
& call for the peace
no other name

TODAY'S STOMACH ACHE

sometimes brain cells
glacially won't function
for oddities of reasons
none of which
are good

sometimes brain cells
divert attention span
from what is at hand
to oddities that
do not matter

sometimes brain cells
cause stomach pains
for responding not
to today's
time frame

UNDER A TREE

under a tree, an hour to go
the sky is cloudy, soon it'll let go
feel the breeze, metaphoric breeze
as soon the birds land on my toes
i'll know the realm of quietest woods
& never go
for home will be here
under this canopy cloud
within the Universe
as deer, squirrel, rabbits do
even spiders and snakes
& i think i'll take my legs
& settle to the ground
fresh virgin to the plow ground
& become a rock
a hard flint rock, the kind mountains
are made of
then as i look up
i'll know growth from childhood to man
is gold well panned
for any human & you
can be & is one with nature
one with Universe
from this blade of grass to Andromeda Galaxy
& i'll sit here under this tree
knowing it could rain in an hour

FREE WATERMELON

"Yo... all you kids out there look this way"
"free watermelon"
he ducked as hundreds of kids
came running his way...

well not a hundred
but forty
well twenty
seemed like thousands
a deluge on a hot sunday afternoon
a waterfall of hot thirsty youngin's
running straight at him
in August
at the quarter midget racetrack

WELL I WAS...

been thinkin' & wonderin'
'bout you
just the thoughts float
the thoughts grasp &
came to ask

how ya doin' this week so
far on Monday morning?

EVAPORATION

ears not hearing
words above their head
are droplets of water evaporated
not available for nourishing
life awaiting
to abound & grow

OBJECTION

objectively
saw this week
had passed beneath
the being on the move
who never quit
but sure got set
back a ledge
or two…

Renaissance

a century slipped past
the concepts so vast
slept & wept
no more songs
written for the wrongs
it all became dollars
red state wallows
society hollows
so sorry folks
the renaissance
did not last

Pitiful Soul

Oh pitiful soul
of such residing goal
lost in the rising
of a sun never setting
while with the speed of light
rolling technology's delight
the sole remaining
superpower
continually calling itself
names from within
let greed
like the speed of light
take control
& flow

JUST DOESN'T

bug eats bug
while mud dries
into pies

but why oh why
do human folk
hate & fight
so much?

just doesn't
make sense
in what
universe really
is...

CAT WAS RIGHT

cat was right
when walking straight up & over
the desk top papers
sitting right here face to face
between keyboard & me
eye to eye

cat was right
i'm here now
pay attention to the moment
papers do not matter
sitting right here face to face
between keyboard & me
cat was right

pay attention
to now

ANOTHER FUNERAL

cells of the body
still electrons possess
no longer swirling
with life force mass

something has broken
the electrical flow
circuit is incomplete
life force has gone on

eyes wide open
eyes now closed
memories are somewhere
the mass of the soul

THE BEGIN BEGAN
LATER STILL

when brane met brain
holographic mind became
you & me & all before
as well as you & me
here & after & later & now
in the illusion
of time moving

MOST BEST

incredibly beneath
the grains of sand
of original hope
so long ago

kinda really sad
how so many things
went so bad

ancient aliens
bigfoot tracking
myth lies building

the misinformation

history rewritten

now a mr ed rerun
is the most best
truthful factual
television show

Ring the Bell

Southwestern Roasted Pecans & Peppers

Yucatan Potato Soup

Frangelico Hazelnut Braised Pork Loin
Peanut Sauce of course
Cinnamon Nutmeg Sweet Potatoes
w/ Butternut Squash & Raisin Swirls
Brunoise Zucchini/Turnips
cupped on Sugar Snap Pea stars

Caramelized Onion & Black Olive Dinner Roll Filled
w/ Cheddar

Intermezzo:
Pate a Choux Banana Pastry Cream Bite

Flourless Chocolate Torte
Whipped Cream Rosette
& Raspberry Sauce garnish

multiple course dinner
for all the guests
All Beverage Salute
the enjoyment

of
methodically altered
molecules
of universe
called cuisine

UNATTENDED

the hot laps
are over

responsibility begins
thru the eyes
which you look

time does not wait
for the
unattended

HURRY

hurry it on up
but not really
just slow it down
watch the sun rise
biding time in a flash of time
hurry it on up
want to find out how the movie ends
but not really
biding time in a flash of time
jumpy as a catnipped cat
just slow it down
watch the sun rise
enjoy time

HAPPY BIRTHDAY

'tis the day
the earth stood still
'tis the day
a new epoch appeared
'tis the day
you were born
'tis the day
the very anniversary day
this ole earth rotates
in brand new ways
happy birthday
this very day

HISTORICAL GEOLOGICAL FORMATION

long eons from now
when paleontologists review
the layers of the earth
showing historical climate change

there will be an odd one named
the Inhofe Layer

filled with second hand smoke
& plastic bag totes
in a deformed carbonated growth
with red emoticons
permeated with
    innately formed brain cells
        long extinct from incorrect usage

OVER THERE

somehow detached
i left my mind
today
River Away became
reality

strangely vibrating
strings converging
time momentarily moving

inner Reason of morality
dispersing flowing

i brought my mind
with me
but i didn't come
along

until later

ALCOHOL

in the deepest crevice
the earth provides
remains this place
to reside
& i
accepted the fate
in which i alone
decided
to participate

misplaced

the smell so well emboldened
me, myself, & i
were forgotten
for the taste
the effects
the numbness of its humor
the un-fun of its wisdom
the ill-defined bravery
like a sad rumor in the mind
& convinced was i
this is happy

JOURNEY TO THE TRAVELERS

a beauty was filled
a glory was offered
    the journey thru the forest
    remains unknown to the travelers
so many roads have forks she
asked plainly who could see
    the forest for the trees
i see infinity i see an atom
    do you know the axe of experience
    will not clear the forest
                for those within
the forest

NOT THE ONLY ONE

knowing the stolen won't be returned
for it be very insignificant
for the local sheriff
to return the
phone
call
showing
all watching
the legal proceeding
again how the little fellas
have no representation & are burned

COLD DAY

it was a cold
day in hell
the first one in quite a spell

The great Satan
Put his sign on the churchyard marquee

"well so much
for global warming"
He decried
to all who passed by

It is difficult
to notice a heat differential

When your feet
stir the very coals
of the fire

No Other Choice

no meant to be
nor should be
is allowed
in universal
free choice
free will

cannot conflict

cannot restrict

right nor wrong
black nor white
grey in rainbows

reflect all options
in free choice

no other choice

TATTERED FELLA

the tattered fella asked
''but don't you really see''
the whiteboard lady spoke
''erase all this for me
there is no other way
both can be so far away''

the atom split ever smaller
hidden vastness spoke
''only two?'' the fella asked
''you think way too small''

NOT BEFORE

the sun rose today
shined upon me
said good morning
good soul

this day you will know
something
you did not know
before

DONE DID

done did
for years on end
a dead end
seemingly with no end

should've known
did know
but kept on anyways
dummy...

FEED 'EM

racecars
are an odd
bunch of critters
worthy of
keeping
well fed

FORMULA

what is the mathematical formula for
pain
happiness
joy
sadness

what is the chemical aberration for
recognition
consciousness
right / wrong
love

the width of the line
is way too wide

not gonna cut it
inside

HIDDEN

unused infinity pieces
enthrall
awaiting
your arrival

Rumpled Conversation

the vagueness began
as each vocal chord
allowed oxygen
vibrations
to occur
in odd sequences
of sentences
ill-constructed
with ideas
randomly
presented
inaccurately

OH NOTHING

nothing is something
some folks are thinking
with nihilist speakism
hidden materialism
regressive taxation

nothing is something
folks keep hiding
in social planning
done in class defining
by calling it something else

I

the i in oneself
is easily seen
as more important
than the i
in every one else

& you already
know it
isn't

PET PEEVES

irritates me so
cup overflowed
emptied on the floor
words of wisdom wasted
time's been a-wasted
screaming dogs
rambling thoughts
ouch & ouch & ouch

let it go
on
& away

YEP

oh yeah want to
oh yeah don't want to
oh yeah want to
oh yeah don't want to
wonder
which'll it be

RED SKY

the day I die
the earth shall spin
like it's been doing
for a few years now

& if there are
clouds in the east
the next morning
then the rays shall be red
just like always

SKIPPED ROCK

What was how far
before or after time
"iota" he spoke
"less than that even"
but whoa
who really knows
how far you can skip a rock on a smooth pond?

COMFORT

Ohhhh stubbed my little toe
thru my foot thru the knee
to well 'round this ole hip
a wrench of pain
no x-ray can explain

high dollar office chair broken
hip workin' like a game token
but I'll tell you what
that jar of cherries sure tasted
like my grandmother just handed them to me

UNIVERSAL

'tis not the structure
of universal matter
'tis rather the nature
in thoughtful chatter

'tis in the love
from way too subtle
'tis not mathematical
rather poetical

universal being
inner photon seeing
things not there
deeply in here

Yellow Stripe

the yellow stripe
up my back
emerged
into the deep blue blood
of richness

knowing it
can be done

Another

attached to the rails
riding the train
imagined the hells
gutting the brain

then woke up
then got up
did my thing

only to
realize

just another day
to
replace an ink cartridge

ENTITY

an entire entity
universally engulfed
entwined in actuality
experiencing inequities
anticipating eventuality
expressing abstractions
in angry obtuse angles
eventually evolves
into
entire entity

THE DOLLARS

it wasn't about the money
the dollars
or the quarters glued to the sidewalk
never was
never ever really was
'cept for the food
for family
& home & friends
& dogs & cats & poems
the daily newspaper & npr radio
& for sure an occasional racecar

it wasn't about the money
never was